Notes on the Delinquent
and the Damned

How can you tell them to be good...th be bad!

This advertising tease was created for a 1956 film called *Crime in the Streets*, but it just as easily could have been used for any of the hundreds of low-budget "exploitation" pictures about lost, lonely, and/or vicious lads and lasses that were produced between 1949 and 1961. During the golden years of the Bad Boys and Wayward Women genres, any lurid headline could inspire a dozen films, which would play either on the bottom half of double bills in the theaters, or solely at drive-ins. These B movies starred such now-forgotten actors as Brett Halsey, Lori Nelson, Yvonne Lime, Mark Damon, Cleo Moore, Fay Spain, and Gary Clarke. Once in a while, someone on the way to something better would pop up—someone like Jack Nicholson, John Cassavetes, Sal Mineo, Robert Vaughn, Yvette Mimieux.

If you haven't heard of most of the films featured in this collection, don't feel bad: Except for occasional appearances on the late-late show, these pictures have barely surfaced since their release thirty-odd years ago. But the wonder of the ever-expanding market for home video holds out new hope that *Blonde Bait, Man Crazy, Dragstrip Riot,* and the others may be "rescued" for a new generation of fans. Till then, remember: "Parents may be shocked, but youth will understand!"

—*Michael Barson*

Special thanks to Michael Sterling and J. H. Beal for sound counsel, and to my editor, David Sternbach, who never saw a chicken-race he didn't like. I also wish to acknowledge the inspiration of Michael Weldon's epochal *The Psychotronic Encyclopedia of Film*.

Note: Because these postcards are oversize, they need the same postage as a first-class letter.

Manufactured in Japan
9876543

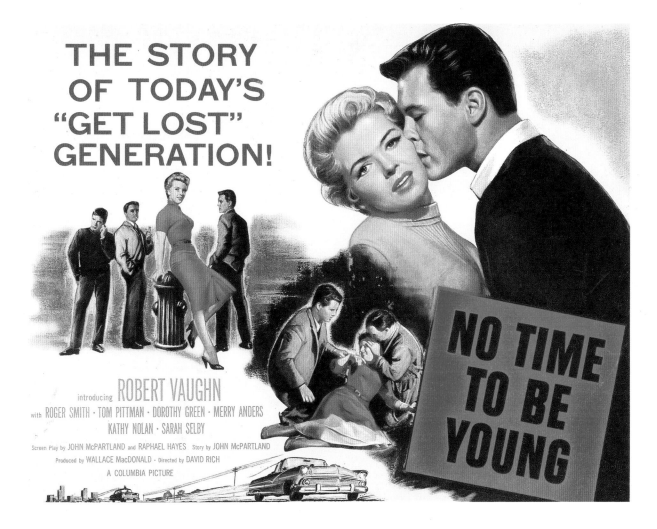

No Time to Be Young (Columbia Pictures, 1957)   Robert (*Man from U.N.C.L.E.*) Vaughn gets top billing in this tale of three lads who hold up a supermarket and suffer severe difficulties with officers of the law thereafter. The fellow mashing his nose into the blonde's cheekbone is Roger Smith, who went on to star in *77 Sunset Strip* and later married Ann-Margret. Which proves that rehabilitation of juvenile offenders is not only possible, but highly desirable.

Bold! Blunt! Brutal!

TODAY'S MOST SEARCHING STORY OF YOUTH...
WRITTEN IN SHAME AND SHOCK, TEARS
AND TRAGEDY, TRUTH AND TERROR!

Man Crazy

starring NEVILLE BRAND · Christine WHITE · Irene ANDERS · Coleen MILLER · John BROWN

with JOE TURKEL · KAREN STEELE · JACK LARSEN · BILL LUNDMARK · JOHN CRAWFORD · OTTOLA NESMITH · CHARLES VICTOR · FRANCES OSBORNE · Narrated by ROBERT BICE

Written and Produced by SIDNEY HARMON and PHILIP YORDAN · Directed by IRVING LERNER · A SECURITY PICTURES PRODUCTION
Released by 20th CENTURY-FOX

Man Crazy (20th Century-Fox, 1953)   Before there were juvenile delinquents, there were Bad Girls. Not bad *evil*—just bad *misguided*. In this tawdry passion play, three girls whose parents weren't paying enough attention light out for Hollywood after finding a pile of cash. Once they fall into the clutches of perennial slug Neville Brand, they regret ever having cut Home Ec.

LOST, LONELY, & VICIOUS · PANTHEON BOOKS · © 1988 · MICHAEL BARSON

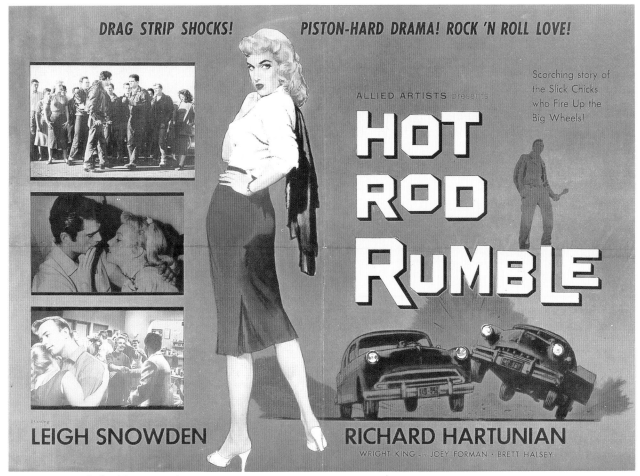

Hot Rod Rumble (Allied Artists, 1957)   At last: The true, unadorned story of "the slick chicks who fire up the big wheels." Seventy-nine minutes of "piston-hard drama" (the best kind) about the rewards and perils of conducting illegal drag races. "You'll need shock absorbers," the ad warned. But whatever happened to Leigh Snowden?

LOST, LONELY, & VICIOUS · PANTHEON BOOKS · © 1988 · MICHAEL BARSON

ROCK BABY ROCK IT

ROCK WITH THE CALYPSO HIT "HEY, JUANITA"

A FREEBAR RELEASE ★ PRODUCED BY J. G. TIGER

Rock Baby, Rock It (Freebar Distributing Co., 1957)   Ultra-low-budget exploitation pic shot in Dallas that relied on local talent. Plot: Gangsters try to take over teen hangout for conversion into seedy nightclub. No way, Horace. The rooster was also a local.

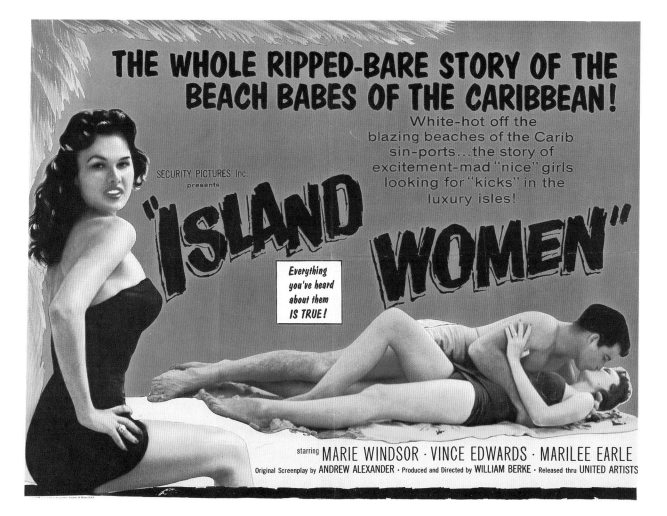

Island Women (United Artists, 1958)   "Everything you've heard about them is true!" I thought so. Rumors that this sensitive drama is now screened for inner-circle execs at Club Med have never been proven conclusively. Vince Edwards turned in his swim trunks to don the white tunic a few years later in *Ben Casey*.

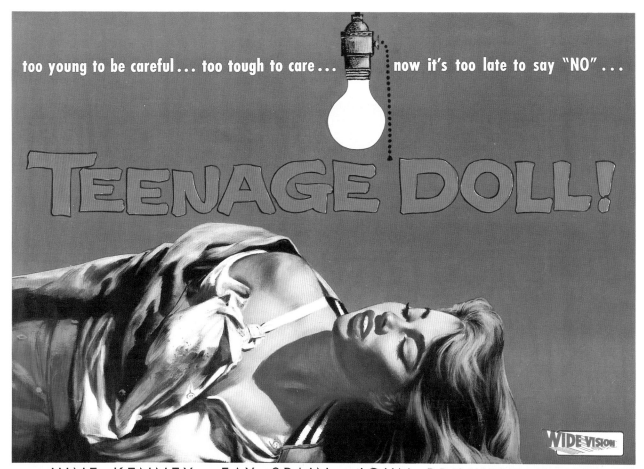

Teenage Doll! (Allied Artists, 1957)   Advertised as "The scorching truth about today's thrill-mad hellcats!" this is one of Roger Corman's darker essays on the awful things kids do to each other in the name of love, lust, and territory. All about rival gangs the Vandals (and female chapter the Vandalettes) and the Tarantulas (and their Black Widows), with "Doll" June Kenney caught in the middle.

Lost, Lonely, and Vicious (Howco International, 1959) "The brightest stars of tomorrow" seem to have faded without a trace after this "confidential exposé" was released. Maybe they shouldn't have kept it so confidential. But who among us cannot warm to this touching tale of boys and girls clawing their way to the top in Hollywood?

BOY
SLAVES

Boy Slaves (RKO Radio Pictures, 1939)   From the same glorious year that gave us *The Wizard of Oz, Gone with the Wind,* and *Mr. Smith Goes to Washington* comes this exposé of child-labor camps—in this case, a turpentine plant. Sounds a lot more provocative than it probably was, which is the whole point of exploitation pictures. But the next time you open a can of turpentine, just stop and think…

RUNNING WILD

TEEN-AGE...
TOUGH...
and TEMPTED
BY EASY MONEY

Hear the hit parade tune
that's sweeping the country
BILL HALEY AND HIS COMETS'
"RAZZLE-DAZZLE"

STARRING
WILLIAM CAMPBELL • MAMIE Van DOREN • KEENAN WYNN • KATHLEEN CASE
with Jan Merlin • John Saxon • Chris Randall • Walter Coy
DIRECTED BY ABNER BIBERMAN • SCREENPLAY BY LEO TOWNSEND • PRODUCED BY HOWARD PINE • A UNIVERSAL-INTERNATIONAL PICTURE

Running Wild (Universal Pictures, 1955)   "The first jolting story of organized teenage gangs," who steal cars for career criminal Keenan Wynn. Mamie van Doren graduated to headline status after her sizzling supporting role here. After supplying the classic "Rock Around the Clock" as the anthem of 1954's *The Blackboard Jungle*, Bill Haley and His Comets were tapped this time for "Razzle-Dazzle."

LOST, LONELY, & VICIOUS · PANTHEON BOOKS · © 1988 · MICHAEL BARSON

DANGER!.. THESE GIRLS ARE HOT!

J. FRANCIS WHITE and JOY HOUCK present

JAIL BAIT

WITH

DOLORES FULLER · LYLE TALBOT
STEVE REEVES · THEODORA THURMAN

AND

JOHN MARTIN · MONA McKINNON
SCOTT McCLOUD · TIMOTHY FARRELL
BUD OSBORNE

Original Screenplay by ALEX GORDON
and EDWARD D. WOOD, Jr.

Produced and Directed by
EDWARD D. WOOD, Jr.

A HOWCO PRODUCTION

Jail Bait (Howco International, 1954)   An almost incoherent crime opus from director-producer-writer Edward D. Wood, Jr., the idiot savant who unleashed cult monuments *Plan 9 from Outer Space* and *Glen or Glenda?* as well as quintessential Bad Girl flick, *The Violent Years*. Dolores Fuller, Wood's first wife, acted in most of his films, and later penned lyrics for such Elvis tunes as "Do the Clam." Like all Wood creations, this is unique, awful, and great.

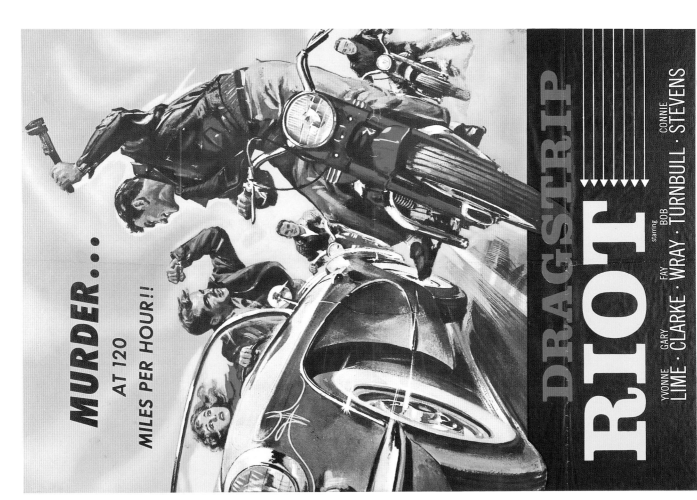

Dragstrip Riot (AIP, 1958)   Features Connie (*Hawaiian Eye*) Stevens, once and future queen of Brooklyn; Gary Clarke, soon to explode into further non-fame in *Date Bait*; Yvonne Lime, star of both *High School Hellcats* and *Speed Crazy*; and Fay Wray, the object of King Kong's affections way back in 1933. But what it all boils down to is this: hot rods versus motorcycles. Hint—keep your eye on that monkey-wrench.

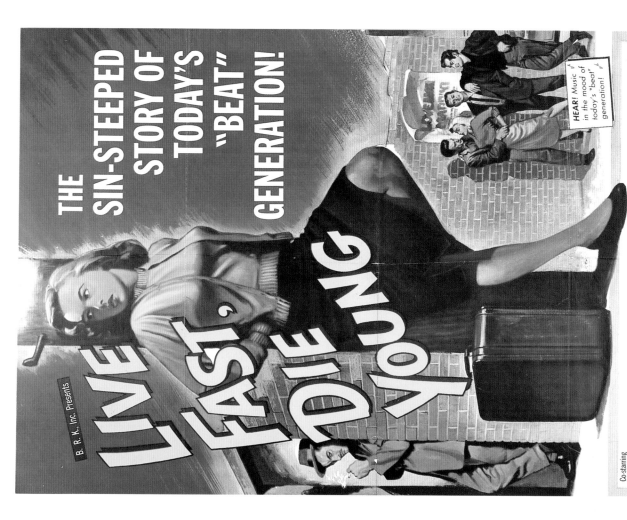

Live Fast, Die Young (Universal Pictures, 1958)   Question: what happened to Ingrid Bergman and Paul Heinreid after they flew off together at the end of *Casablanca*? Answer: Bergman bore an illegitimate daughter to film director Roberto Rossellini, while Heinreid became a director of B movies like this one. With Mike (*Mannix*) Connors, Mary (*The Wild One*) Murphy, and Troy (*Surfside 6*) Donahue. "The road she travels is a one-way highway to hell!"

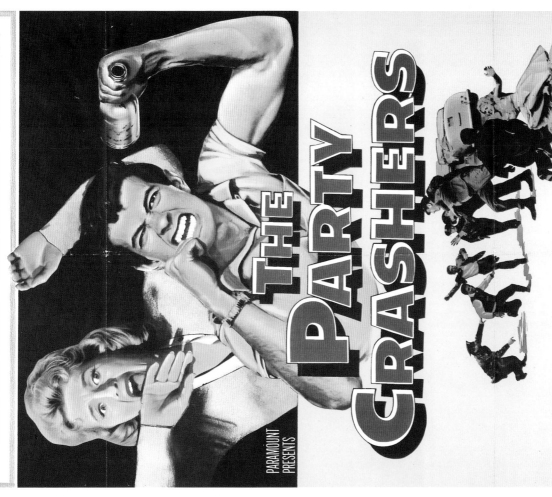

WHO ARE THE DELINQUENTS —
KIDS OR THEIR "RESPECTABLE" PARENTS?

PARAMOUNT PRESENTS

THE PARTY CRASHERS

STARRING

CONNIE STEVENS · ROBERT DRISCOLL · MARK DAMON · FRANCES FARMER · DORIS DOWLING

PRODUCED BY WILLIAM ALLAND · DIRECTED BY BERNARD GIRARD

SCREENPLAY BY BERNARD GIRARD AND DAN LUNDBERG

FROM A STORY BY WILLIAM ALLAND AND DAN LUNDBERG

The Party Crashers (Paramount Pictures, 1958)   "Kids running wild because their parents run wilder!" Sure. Mark (*Life Begins at 17*) Damon is a hood, Connie Stevens is a nice girl, and they end up at a fancy motel bash from which Damon's alcoholic mother is tossed out on her ear. Lovely 1930s star Frances Farmer, who suffered a nervous breakdown and was institutionalized by her mother, tried to make a comeback here. It didn't take.

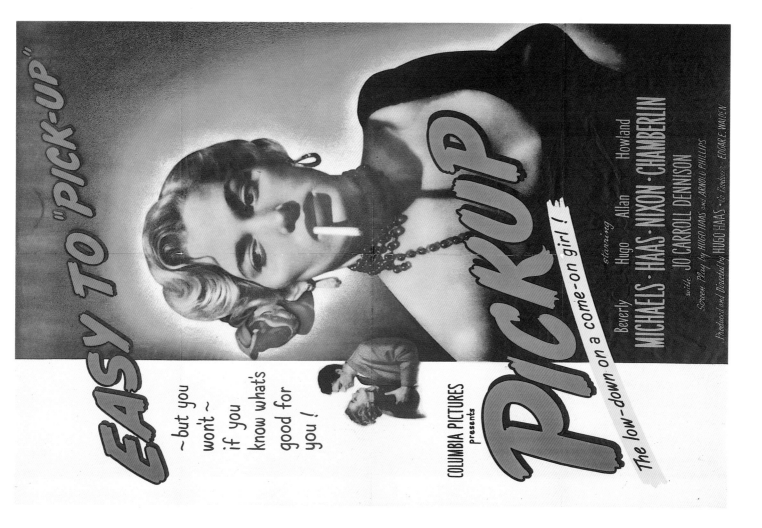

Pickup (Columbia Pictures, 1951)   Innocent man duped by conniving blonde—the favorite plot of former character actor Hugo Haas, who became the Orson Welles of B movies during the 1950s. He wrote, directed, produced, and sometimes acted in such sordid melodramas as *Bait, The Girl on a Bridge, Edge of Hell, Hold Back Tomorrow,* and *Paradise Alley.* The titles say it all.

CAR CRAZY!...
SPEED CRAZY!...
BOY CRAZY!...

DRAGSTRIP GIRL

with Hollywood's Newest TEENAGE STARS:

FAY SPAIN · STEVE TERRELL
JOHN ASHLEY · FRANK GORSHIN

A GOLDEN STATE PRODUCTION
Produced by ALEX GORDON
Executive Producer: SAMUEL Z. ARKOFF
Screenplay by LOU RUSOFF
Directed by EDWARD L. CAHN
AN AMERICAN-INTERNATIONAL PICTURE

Dragstrip Girl (AIP, 1957)   Fay Spain competes on the chicken-run circuit against John Ashley—but don't blame him; with her helmet on, she looked like a guy. Frank Gorshin, the Riddler on the campy *Batman* TV series of the 1960s, made his mark in other drive-in faves like *Invasion of the Saucer Man* and *Hot Rod Girl*. This was on a double bill with *Rock All Night*.

Betrayed Women (Allied Artists, 1955)   A women-in-prison yarn that really sticks to your ribs. Beverly (*Pickup*) Michaels, Carole (*Female Fiends*) Mathews, and Peggy Knudson crash out of a Louisiana jail after suffering indignities at the hands of nasty guard Sara Haden. Lawyer Tom Drake—remember him as Judy's apple-cheeked suitor in *Meet Me in St. Louis*?—is dragged into the swamps as their hostage. He probably didn't even mind.

LOST, LONELY, & VICIOUS · PANTHEON BOOKS · © 1988 · MICHAEL BARSON

Why do so many rich girls go so wrong?

SHE had a knife!

SHE toyed with men!

SHE played with matches!

COLUMBIA PICTURES presents

Problem Girls

starring Helen Walker · Ross Elliott · Susan Morrow · Written and Priced by AUBREY WISBERG and JACK POLLEXFEN · Directed by E.A.DUPONT

Problem Girls (Columbia Pictures, 1953) "Nothing can tame them... Scandal can't shame them...Newspapers can't name them!" All right: Why *do* so many rich girls go so wrong? And does turning the hose on them *truly* rehabilitate them? Concerned Americans want to know. Released on a double bill with *One Girl's Confession* as "two sensational girl shows."

A GIRL DELINQUENT ...A JET PROPELLED GANG.... OUT FOR FAST KICKS!

JUVENILE JUNGLE

in NATURAMA

STARRING

COREY ALLEN · REBECCA WELLES
RICHARD BAKALYAN
ANNE WHITFIELD · JOE DI REDA

with JOE CONLEY · WALTER COY · TAGGART CASEY

Directed by WILLIAM WITNEY Written by ARTHUR T. HORMAN

Produced by SIDNEY PICKER REPUBLIC PICTURES Presents A CORONADO Production

Juvenile Jungle (Republic Pictures, 1958)   Corey Allen leads his sociopathic pals on a kidnapping that's supposed to net them 40 grand. But he falls in love with his captive, as so often happens, and several violent actions then occur. Only a film processed in "Naturama" could do justice to this story. Gang member Richard Bakalyan was also terrific in *The Cool and the Crazy* as a high-school student addicted to pot.

"I confess
I'm the kind of
girl every
man wants–
but shouldn't
marry!"
COLUMBIA PICTURES
presents
One Girl's
Confession
STARRING
CLEO MOORE · HUGO HAAS · GLENN LANGAN
Written, Produced and Directed by HUGO HAAS

One Girl's Confession (Columbia Pictures, 1953)   Trash with philosophical pretensions, and thus special. Director-writer-producer-actor Hugo Haas created a dozen strange morality plays, most featuring bottle-blonde bombshells Beverly Michaels and Cleo Moore as betraying women who find redemption. Haas and Moore teamed up for their moth-and-flame routine again in *Hit and Run*.

Girl Gangs That STOP AT NOTHING!

JEWELL ENTERPRISES, INC. PRESENTS

GIRLS ON THE LOOSE

Starring MARA CORDAY · LITA MILAN · also starring MARK RICHMAN
BARBARA BOSTOCK

Directed by PAUL HENREID Screenplay by ALAN FRIEDMAN, DOROTHY RAISON and ALLEN RIVKIN
Produced by HARRY RYBNICK and RICHARD KAY Associate Producer EDWARD B. BARISON
A UNIVERSAL-INTERNATIONAL RELEASE

Girls on the Loose (Universal Pictures, 1958)   "Trigger tough and ready for *anything!*" A payroll robbery is nothing new—unless it's carried off by a gang of teenage hellcats. But before they can decide how to spend their $200,000 haul, the impetuous lasses kill each other. Still, it must have seemed like a vacation to Mara Corday, who had recently tangled with gigantic mutant bugs in *Tarantula* and *The Black Scorpion*.

Women of The Caves 1000 Years From Now!

CAPTIVE WOMEN

GLORIA **SAUNDERS** · RON **RANDELL**

Directed by STUART GILMORE

starring ROBERT **CLARKE** · MARGARET **FIELD**

Written and Produced by AUBREY WISBERG and JACK POLLEXFEN

R K O RADIO PICTURES

Captive Women (RKO Radio Pictures, 1952)   New York in the twenty-ninth century is almost as much of a mess as it is now. A post-atomic society has evolved, with the peaceful Mutes being harassed by the violent Norms. No mention of mortgage rates; otherwise, quite accurate. Also released as *1000 Years from Now*.

ALIMONY RACKETEERS PREY
ON INNOCENT DUPES!

A Pretty Face
A Shapely Figure
—She Used Them
To Get What
She Wanted!

ALIMONY

Starring

MARTHA VICKERS
JOHN BEAL
HILLARY BROOKE

introducing

LAURIE LIND

LEONID KINSKY · DOUGLASS DUMBRILLE
RALPH GRAVES · JAMES GUILFOYLE
MARIE BLAKE

Produced by Constantin J. David
Associate Producer Anthony Z. Landi
Directed by Alfred Zeisler
Screenplay by Lawrence Lipton,
George Bricker, Sherman L. Lowe
Original Story by Sherman L. Lowe
and Royal K. Cole
An Equity Picture
An Eagle Lion Films Release

Alimony (Eagle-Lion Films, 1949)   Another film in need of video resurrection. Only three years earlier, Martha Vickers was trying to seduce Humphrey Bogart in *The Big Sleep*. Now this. The Eagle-Lion company distributed a number of now-forgotten B pictures after absorbing poverty-row studio PRC in 1947; but in 1951 they were themselves bought out by United Artists. *Sic transit...*

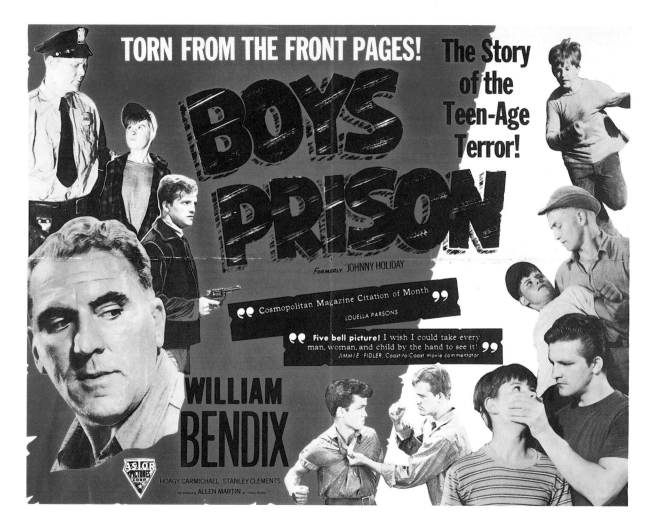

Boys' Prison (Astor Pictures reissue, circa 1954)   Best known for his long-running TV sit-com *The Life of Riley*, William Bendix here plays a hard-boiled retired cavalry officer who rehabilitates JD-in-training Johnny Holiday. Filmed on location at the Indiana Boy's School in Bloomington. Less sappy than the Boys' Town films with Mickey Rooney and Spencer Tracy, but hardly "Teen-Age Terror." Hoagy Carmichael sings a Christmas song to the little darlings.

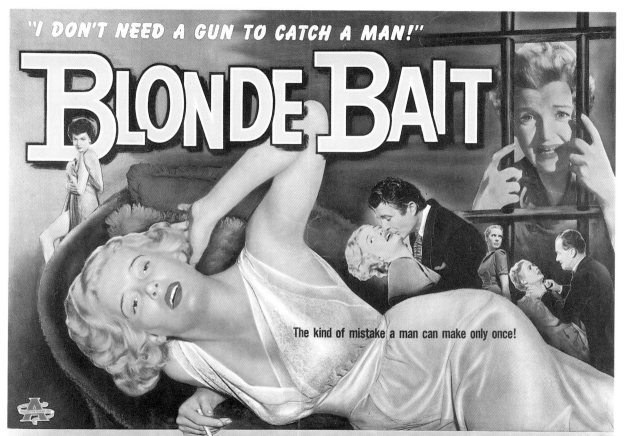

Blonde Bait (Associated Film Releasing Corp. 1956)   Originally released in Britain as *Women Without Men*, this was reshot with American actors in certain scenes and retitled for U.S. distribution. Beverly Michaels, already an expert in prison breakouts from *Betrayed Women*, escapes this time from an English house of correction. Maybe she just doesn't like institutional chow.

"UNTAMED YOUTH"

STARRING THE GIRL BUILT LIKE A PLATINUM POWERHOUSE MAMIE VAN DOREN · LORI NELSON PRESENTED BY WARNER BROS.

Untamed Youth (Warner Bros., 1957)   "The Girl Built Like a Platinum Powerhouse," Mamie Van Doren, was the preeminent 1950s icon of peroxide perfection. A few of her triumphs: *Girls Town, High School Confidential*, and *The Beat Generation*. Here she suffers the advances of lecherous John Russell, the director of the "punishment farm" where Mamie and her sister (Lori Nelson) have been sent for hitchhiking without a license. Rock great Eddie Cochran has a singing cameo.

LOST, LONELY, & VICIOUS · PANTHEON BOOKS · © 1988 · MICHAEL BARSON

Female Fiends (Cinema Associates, 1959)   How did a perfectly respectable mystery novel from the 1940s, *Puzzle for Fiends* by Patrick Quentin, turn into this shamelessly exploitative vehicle for erstwhile Tarzan Lex Barker? Let us simply give thanks.

BODY OF A BOY!

MIND OF A MONSTER!

SOUL
OF AN
UNEARTHLY
THING!

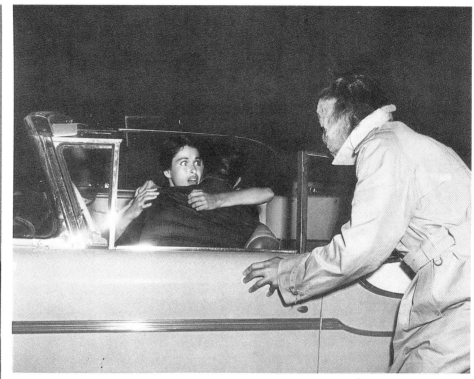

I WAS A TEENAGE FRANKENSTEIN

starring
WHIT BISSELL · PHYLLIS COATES
ROBERT BURTON · GARY CONWAY

Produced by
HERMAN COHEN

Directed by   Screenplay by
HERBERT L. STROCK · KENNETH LANGTRY

A JAMES H. NICHOLSON-SAMUEL Z. ARKOFF PRODUCTION
AN AMERICAN INTERNATIONAL PICTURE

I Was a Teenage Frankenstein (AIP, 1957)   "Body of a boy! Mind of a Monster! Soul of an Unearthly Thing!" Puberty *is* hell, especially for Gary Conway. This cheesy exercise was rushed into production to cash in on the success of Michael Landon's *I Was a Teenage Werewolf*. Landon's condition was cured, of course, and he moved out west to the Ponderosa. If only Lorne Greene had adopted Gary...

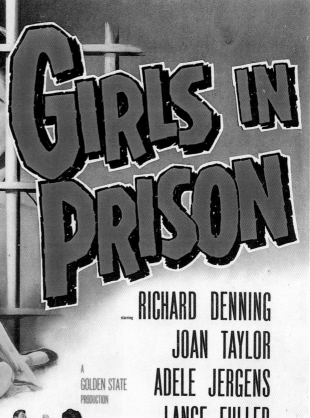
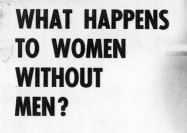

WHAT HAPPENS TO WOMEN WITHOUT MEN?

THE SHOCKING STORY OF ONE MAN AGAINST 1000 WOMEN!

GIRLS IN PRISON

A GOLDEN STATE PRODUCTION

starring

RICHARD DENNING
JOAN TAYLOR
ADELE JERGENS
LANCE FULLER

Executive Producer, SAMUEL Z. ARKOFF · Directed by EDWARD L. CAHN
Produced by ALEX GORDON · Screenplay by LOU RUSOFF

Girls in Prison (AIP, 1956)   Richard Denning is wildly miscast as a sympathetic priest, while Jane Darwell, who won an Oscar in 1940 for *The Grapes of Wrath*, seems very tired as the matron of this sorry joint. From the director of *Riot in Juvenile Prison, Shake, Rattle, and Rock,* and *Dragstrip Girl.*

LOST, LONELY, & VICIOUS · PANTHEON BOOKS · © 1988 · MICHAEL BARSON

Blonde Ice (Film Classics, 1948)   Low-budget film-noir that has not been shown on late-night TV in many a moon. Why? What are they trying to hide? Do they really think we'd rather watch reruns of *Barnaby Jones*?

PREHISTORIC
REBELS
against
PREHISTORIC
MONSTERS!

TEENAGE CAVEMAN

Starring ROBERT VAUGHN · DARRAH MARSHALL · LESLIE BRADLEY

Produced and Directed by ROGER CORMAN · Screenplay by R. WRIGHT CAMPBELL · A JAMES H. NICHOLSON & SAMUEL Z. ARKOFF Production · An AMERICAN-INTERNATIONAL Picture

Teenage Caveman (AIP, 1958)   Yes, it's Robert Vaughn again, hot on the heels of his triumphant tandem, *Unwed Mother* and *No Time to Be Young*. As you can see from this dramatic scene, no expense was spared either in special effects or in archery lessons for Vaughn. ("Less limp with the wrist, Bobby!") The shock ending would be echoed a decade later in *Planet of the Apes*.

LOST, LONELY, & VICIOUS · PANTHEON BOOKS · © 1988 · MICHAEL BARSON

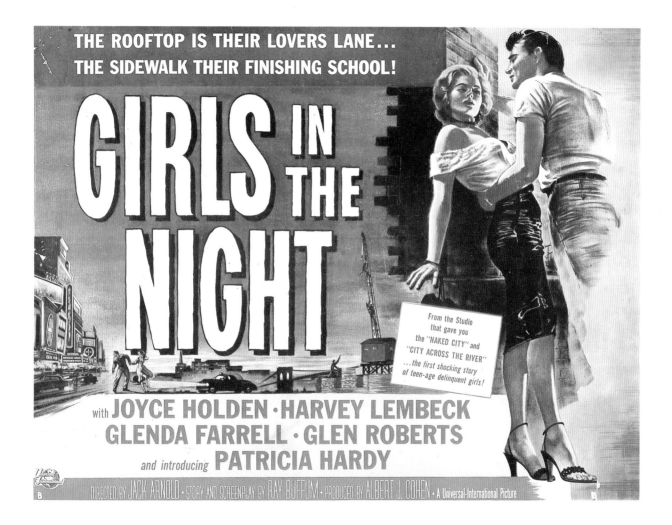

Girls in the Night (Universal Pictures, 1953)   A downbeat look at New York tenement life. Director Jack Arnold would later score with such sci-fi classics as *The Incredible Shrinking Man, It Came from Outer Space,* and *The Creature from the Black Lagoon.* Cast member Harvey Lembeck appears as motorcycle gang leader Eric Von Zipper in the Annette *Beach Party* films of the 1960s. "The first shocking story of teenage delinquent girls"—but not the last, thank God.